Poems
by a Regular Guy

SCOTT BOURNE

authorHOUSE®

AuthorHouse™
1663 Liberty Drive
Bloomington, IN 47403
www.authorhouse.com
Phone: 1 (800) 839-8640

Published by AuthorHouse 02/11/2015

ISBN: 978-1-4969-6926-2 (sc)
ISBN: 978-1-4969-6925-5 (e)

Print information available on the last page.

Any people depicted in stock imagery provided by Thinkstock are models,
and such images are being used for illustrative purposes only.
Certain stock imagery © Thinkstock.

This book is printed on acid-free paper.

Because of the dynamic nature of the Internet, any web addresses or
links contained in this book may have changed since publication and
may no longer be valid. The views expressed in this work are solely those
of the author and do not necessarily reflect the views of the publisher,
and the publisher hereby disclaims any responsibility for them.

This book is dedicated to the Boston Bruins for their blue collar heart. To Jerry Garcia for his inspiration that he spread through his music. And last but not least, my beautiful wife for all her love and support. She found this lost nomad and gave him peace in his heart.

Scott lives in Massachusetts with his wife and two boys. He is a lover of the arts, his favorite hockey team, and good music. Scott enjoys landscaping his yard, writing poetry and will never turn down a good micro-brew.

Contents

Complete

When two people who were meant to be together become lovers and partners, the other parts of their worlds sometime feel like they don't exist, like a blind eye has been turned towards them, making them feel unimportant, outcast in our lives

This is not true though, because without our friends and family we would not be the two people we are, we would not be the special someone that we have become, it is our family and friends who make us who we are, the reason we are together

Our family and friends are part of our special lives, making us stronger by their presence, it is because of them that we met, and it is because of them we love each other, family, for good or bad have shaped the way we think, lived and loved

As our bond and love grows, our relationship with our family and friends will also grow, yes, it will be different, as in all relationships, but we are not complete without good friends and family, just like we are not complete without each other

I Hurt You

I wake this morning with this guilt on my mind, I couldn't sleep, dreams were not to be had, my words had hurt you they screwed with your mind, why something like this happens I can't explain, all I know is that I hurt you and I feel so bad

Because of outside issues that had nothing to do with you, you just were in the wrong place at the wrong time and my anger went right at you, it was not my intention, my insides getting the better of me, I wish I could take it all back but life doesn't let you walk back time

I know this has happened before, outside sources screwing with my mind, things I can't control because the world doesn't work in real time, push that first domino and the world just fucks with my mind and in the end I just hurt the one who is on my side

I wish I could control the anger when it builds up inside, like an erupting volcano with my feelings right at the top spewing from all sides, I know it sounds silly, I should be able to put these feelings aside, but life is not that easy, not everything in life is a sunrise

I can't say sorry enough, I know words are just words until I'm man enough to back their meaning, these words don't even heal my mind, but I promise to try harder to be a better man, I just ask for your forgiveness and ask you to love the man you know and not the man behind the pain

About Us

You will never be mine and I will never be yours but we will both be our own entity, whose roots combine to make a foundation of happiness, trust and oneness which can only make our unity stronger, making us the couple that everyone envies

I want you to be my teacher and I want to teach you, I want you to grow, as I should, which will only make us stronger for each other, learning from each other, feeling free to express ourselves, exposing our souls, making our bond stronger

Finding out about ourselves inside and out allows us to grow so we have more of our souls to share with no labels, no judgments, no basis of ownership, we are one as lovers and friends working on a foundation of happiness for our future lives

Being Happy

Sometimes it takes someone you love to pass away to make you realize what is important, what living is all about, we only get one shot at this whole ball of wax, live it to the fullest, so we die with happiness in our heart

Life is like a business chart with lines going up and down, instead of gains and losses, the lines equate to happiness and sadness, we will all experience sadness, that is something that can't be denied, but happiness is the goal

The charts in our life, when it is all done, I hope that my lines are mostly going up and not down, this should be everyone's goal, which will be my definition if I won the game of life, knowing that I smiled more than frowned

A Dad's Passing

I know your heart is heavy, your dad is gone
but always know, that he loved you so,
the shell we saw at the end was not his definition,
the man you knew will always be in your heart and soul

I know this is not right to say
but he was my favorite of your kin
my favorite because it was he you are most like
he is the reason I fell in love with you

Your warm soul, big heart and your silent persona
like your dad, you don't need to be loud to be heard,
his love was known by you, like your love is known by
our son, you are him in a nutshell, love just falls from
your being

Being loved like you were by your dad is something I envy,
I never had the chance to know what a father's love was,
but watching your father love you the way a father should
and watching your love for him at the end, that's love
with no end

Coming Back In A Song

I was talking the other day, talking about my dear ole mom, my little man asks will she be coming back, I look at him and answer with a smile and laughter and say yes, she will be back in a song, a lullaby to sing you to sleep, a song to keep you safe and put a smile on your face

I sit here wondering what kind of song would I like to come back as, would it be dusty old country song, a move your hips song sung by Marvin Gaye, a sit there and be angry angst song from Seattle, sit there with my eyes closed Coltrane tune, dance my head off with Chuck Berry, or pick up my Sunday paper and sit back to Mr. Mozart

I sit around and smile knowing that I would come back in a long jam that only a San Francisco band could provide, a long wonderful melody, with beautiful lyrics, guitar tones from heaven and a melody filled with love, I'd dance along the musical symbols and lie around on the notes and be happy with my fate

Day to day folks discuss coming back in other forms, other animals, maybe even a chair, but not me, I say they are all wrong, I'm coming back in a song, I'm going to make people dance, smile, laugh, and cry all at the same time, grooving my way into their soul by starting at their toes

Chugging Along

It's just another day, a smile on my face, my wife is beautiful, my boys running from place to place, life is good so I look at the sky and say thank you for my wonderful life and so I keep on chugging along

I watch the planes, I watch the trains, and I hear the cars roar by, everyone in a rush, everyone in a race, trying to get there first, but no not me, I'll take my time, I'll smell the flowers as I walk by, as I keep chugging along

Life is simple, don't make it so hard, love the ones you're with and don't pine for anymore, be happy with what you have because what you've got is well enough, breath in the air, put a smile on your face because that's all you need to keep chugging along

When it's my time to go, I'll accept my fate, I'll thank the all mighty for all that's been put on my plate, I'll look at my wife, I'll look at my sons, a smile will appear on my face, I'll think back on my life knowing all along that I was so happy because I kept chugging along

A Happy Birthday To You

My love, it's that time of year again,
the greatest day of my life, the
day the god said let there be you,
let there be you to save my lost soul

Every year your beauty only grows,
your eyes still melting me every day,
your smile shining the sun on me, warming
me with the warmth that only your love can give

Holding you every night is my goal, everyday
keeping you near me so I can feel your soft
skin, absorbing me into your space, making
me feel that life cannot get any better

The celebration of your life is also the
celebration of our family, if you were missing
there would be no me, no little boys and
most of all, there would be no place to call home

So let's celebrate your birth, celebrate your
love, celebrate your being, celebrate your
motherhood, celebrate everything about you,
but most of all I celebrate that you're my best friend

Dying A Little Every Day

Waking up every morning from the day we arrive, we die a little every day, we're born to die, that's just life, don't fight it, live it, live like every day is your last, live it and love it with a smile on your face

I know by the title you would think this is a sad poem, but oh no you would be wrong, it's just fact that we die a little every day, so go make love to your favorite girl, hug all those that you love and make sure you smile at strangers as you walk by because being mean is such hard work

Looking at my favorite girl I'm so happy that I get to grow old with her, her smile, her eyes, and oh dear lord the way she shakes that thing, I don't mind dying a little every day with her, lying next to her every night and taking all of her in until my heart doesn't beat anymore and I've lost all my breath

Life is to be lived, live it well, smell those roses, taste the rain, go climb the highest mountain, make love as much as you can, hug your loved ones, play hockey and slide on until the next day, we die a little every day and that's okay with me because this is the deal we all made so go out with a smile on your face

Falling In Love Across The Table

Nervous all day, waiting to meet you, our first date was upon us, walking the bean, and looking at you, I could not believe I was really there, then as we ate and I looked at you, I fell in love from across the table

As time went on, dates were in our past, life moved on as our roots came to last, your home, my home, it did not matter, with food all around, with the aroma of things that made us smile, I see you there and I fall in love from across the table

You said yes and we were on our way, our lives becoming intertwined in our own special way, we laid a foundation, we laid our place on earth, we, together, in synch, we sit down to eat, as I fall in love from across the table

We are now four and our life moves on, our two boys living our dream, we teach them the love that used to be just a dream, we add our spices, we add our color and as we sit down to eat I fall in love all over again from across the table

Forgiveness

Forgiveness is a word that I don't believe in, the word isn't even in my dictionary, my moto is to never forgive and forget, I've been burned so many times in my life to forgive everyone who has hurt me, I can't let anyone skate free, those who have sinned against me and the world I live in, I only pray for pain, a pain that moves through their soul like a burning fire

A good Christian would say forgive and forget, let the sins of others be forgotten but I believe in an eye for an eye, look at the world from my eyes and see the things that I've seen, wars with no end, people who get pleasure at hurting others, the rich laugh at the poor, the elderly ignored and if you are different, your pain has no end, and religion has become a tool used by politicians to pit us vs them

Forgiveness is a good idea, it has merit, but no one cares anymore, the world is in a free fall and god stopped caring about us all a long time ago, if my words are false to you, then prove me wrong, show me that love is still all around us and people still care for their fellow man, it is then and only then that I will learn to forgive others and live a life in peace and solitude

Alone

It's dark and dreary, rain coming down, is this really true or is it all in my mind, when all alone, feeling as though no one sees you, do you really exist if no one reaches out to touch you, hold you, to make you feel warm inside, to help put your troubles aside

There have been too many days in my recent past where I have felt that I walk alone, I walk through my streets, I walk through my home, feeling as if there is no one to share my soul, feeling empty inside, having really bad thoughts, does anyone know that I'm even alive

Solitude is fine in some certain times, like sitting in a forest listening to the tress or gazing at a mountain top and feeling its breeze, but when one walks the street of his own hometown feeling like he doesn't belong, no one is watching because he is all alone

The thoughts of loneliness come too often, it's a feeling I'm trying to shake, because I do know I'm loved, this is not unknown, but when one is alone, his mind starts to wander, trying to solve all mankind's problems when he has his own to conquer

God Has
Left The Building

God has left the building and we have no one to blame but mankind, man has fucked up God's greatest creation, killing his earth slowly but surely, killing all its living things as if it was our right, man is its own worst enemy, slowly dying every day

A great philosopher once stated that God used to exist but he disappeared because man used him as a coat, putting him on when needed, taking him off when done, mankind has pissed on his teachings while doing their evil deeds in his name

God has forsaken us because of our selfish ways, politicians and religious figures say they speak for him, especially the most pious, while they start wars and explain they are killing in his name because the bible says so, while they plunge the sword

God has moved on from us, he is no longer in charge, look at the world around us, wars, people killing for the fun of it, people who are different are outcasts, people lie and cheat to get ahead, hide behind our technology and purposely cause others pain

As Mother Nature wreaks havoc all around the world, innocent people dying from the world leaders' egos, people will say God does everything for a reason, well I say you are all wrong, God has had enough of mankind and he has left the building

Is This All There Is

I'm living day to day with debts and bills I know I can't pay, life is so hard at times it pains me to say, some days I stay in bed hoping it all goes away, thinking where is my happiness and wondering if this is all there is

The sun never shines at my end of town, the clouds hang among us with the reaper ready to pounce, I wonder where I went wrong, what did I do that my lord has forsaken me and keeps me wondering if this is all there is

I see happy shiny people all the time, the tube brings them to me through its small little screen, I picture myself in their happy little world, driving their nice cars and wearing their nice clothes then I look at myself wondering if this is all there is

Why are some of us blessed with so much while people like me scrap by with so little, does god have favorites I'd like to know, show me his list and I'll do my best to appear on it while I sit here thinking is this all there is

I ask that I only be treated fairly, I'm a good person you know, I've never harmed anyone, I work myself to the bone, give me a chance, please tell me there is more, let me have hope, let me show I can reach the sky, I can't keep on going if this is all there is

Please tell me there are days between, my days that are now and my days to come, where happiness will shine and love will conquer all, I deserve happiness, I know I can shine, because the life that I have, this can't be the end game, please tell me this isn't all there is

A Door For Each Level

People don't know this, well maybe they do, we pass through many doors for each phase of our life, some have more doors than others, some are more happy and some are more sad, the door that opens for you depends on how you are living your life, were you kind to your neighbor, did you help those in need, or did you just go through life filling your pockets with all your misdeeds.

The door of death is not for you to die, but for you to experience when one close to you passes on, your mom or your dad or maybe your best friend, this door reminds you that all of our lives will one day end, going through this door is just part of life, it's okay to feel sorrow, to miss a loved one you loved so dear, this door can't be ignored, it's part of everyone's fate

The door of compassion is a test to all of us, do we just love those close to us or can we feel other's pain, to try to understand others who do not look like us, think like us or do we turn our backs and watch them suffer in pain, and say it's not our problem, or step up to god's plate and push hate aside

Your door of happiness hopefully opens many times, babies are born, graduations at hand, birthdays and holidays and vacations are planned, being with loved ones, or having a fantastic wife, everyone deserves to go through this door many times in their life

The door of aging opens many times, bringing happiness and sadness, wisdom and joy, learning to share knowledge from one generation to the next, learn from our wrongs so they can get it right, learn from our mistakes that we make at certain ages, laughing at ourselves because we were not always right

There are many doors that open in life, some not of our choosing, do the best that you can when each door appears because at some point in life it will have to be closed, once they are closed they will not open again because the next phase of your life will be here and another door will be opened, kick the door down if you must, make your own fate so the last door you open will be at heaven's gate

I Hate Myself

I hate myself, this is so true
I hate myself, what am I doing here
I hate myself, I'm nowhere close to where I want to be
I hate myself because I don't have a job
I hate myself because of the decisions I've made
I hate myself because I can't do what I want
I hate myself because there is no money in my pockets
I hate myself because of the failure that I am
I hate myself because my future is so unclear
I hate myself because I have nothing to my name
I hate myself because my opinion means nothing
I hate myself because everything I touch turns to shit
I hate myself because I hate my family
I hate myself because all I have is my stupid last name
I hate myself because I feel my life is going up in flames

I can't help the way I feel, it's all in my brain, I walk around every day with so much pain, nothing seems to go my way, all my decisions turn out to be shit day after day

I hate myself because I don't control a damn thing in my life
I hate myself because my bad luck is hurting my family
I hate myself because people come after me for things I didn't do

I hate myself because life just isn't fair
I hate myself because others are controlling my happiness
I hate myself because life is just a living hell
I just fucking hate myself

Addiction

Addiction, I find it the only way
Addiction, I find it helps me fly away
Addiction, the pain is never known to some
Addiction, my children's love just goes away
Addiction, takes out the messiahs among us
Addiction, is known to the rich and poor

Why does the addiction keep fucking up the one's you love?
Why does the addiction mean more to you than your sons and daughters?
Why do you make us suffer and cry from your addiction?

Addiction is the feeling that no one understands
Addiction makes me feel so good inside
Addiction helps me find my selfish side
Addiction is my friend that no one understands
Addiction helps me find my way in the world
Addiction will be with me until the day I die

Now that you are dead and gone, your addiction only makes us mourn
Now that you are dead and gone, your addiction has allowed us to move on

Having Sugar Tonight

Tonight I wander around your bed, looking to see where I should be, under, over maybe even in between, how would that happen I just don't know but all I know by the smile on your face is that I'm going to have sugar tonight

I touch and caress all the right places, you giggle and laugh at all my advances, my awkwardness standing out as if it were my first time, but I still keep my ego and smile right back because I know I'm getting sugar tonight

You give me the sign, saying come right on in, lying on top of me with your silly grin, your smile so bright in the darkest of nights, my favorite parts speaking to me shining so bright, I smile right back because I'm getting sugar tonight

As we lay together all sweaty and tired, we laugh at the sounds that we made together, holding tight and not letting go, I think about your warmness that surrounded me a minute ago and I smile to myself because I got sugar tonight

A Quick Love Poem

Love equals the soul
The soul equals pureness
Pureness of the heart equals beauty
Beauty equals the flower
The flower is you, blooming with life for me

I Love You

I love you in the morning, I love you at night
I love when you yell at me, I love you when we fight
I love you all the time not just during good times
I love you more than anyone I hope you understand

I'm the lost nomad without you in my life, my life is
meaningless without you in my command, you steer me
in all the right directions even when I put up a fight, you
knock me right down with that love in your eyes

I love you on land, I love you on sea,
I love you in the sky, I love you because you love me
I love you for being you, I wouldn't want you any other way
I love your for that smile on your face with those shining
green eyes

Love is a dangerous word, because it needs to go both
ways, but the love you show for me just surrounds me
making it hard to breath, but out of breath is just fine
with me, squeeze me so hard that you fall inside of me.
Your love makes me higher than any drug has ever done
making me feel so free

I love you, because you make me smile every day
I love you and I can't say it any other way
I love you and in case you didn't hear
I love you, I love you, I love you

Love For The Songs

I want to say thank you, and you ask me why, my only reply is for a real good time, you smile in reply that thanks is not needed and that it was they who were most grateful, because without you we would not have been seeded, we were in it together dancing and singing until we played our last song

Our lives have been affected in the most positive ways, as you think we affected yours in the same way, with years of love and following, who could ask for more, you earned all of our roots with music and more, the sound that came straight from the bay, music that made us sway, as we walked through life with a smile every day

A man with the sunshine in his eyes once said that only love could fill and we heard it in the songs that filled our hearts, and we agree that it was the love for the songs over the years, down that lazy river road, good times and happiness, shaking and bopping with no extra load

We all thank you because there was no better adventure that could be had, the last one that has ever been known,

letting us come along for the ride, because without love
in a dream, our dreams would never have come true and
we all dreamed together until that last ride we always
loved you

Love Of War

Behind their rich walls, they plan their wars that no one can see, they don't know how to let it be, the machine that drives them is the color of green, it blinds them and excites them showing their greed

Their friends in Washington, the cowards they all are, they have no problem sending our sons and daughters to war, while protecting their own turning them all into whores, speaking their mind that you don't understand freedom is on the line

The politicians they just love to fight, they use us like pawns, and their backers of rich send them some more, their pockets never empty because of their love of war, the little people like you and me lie dead in the streets never to soar

They love their war machines, driven by us poor, they have no fear because it is not them who fight, but it's the lives of our kin who are sent into battle, no one ever telling that there is no end in sight, the rich get richer on the backs of the poor, it's today's fashion that never goes out of style because their lives don't really matter

A Brand New Day

Waking up in the morning is not the same, my feet glide in Motown ways, my heart beats a little faster, with big ole pumps, love has found me what can I say, a girl with green eyes shows me the way, when I met her it was a brand new day

She holds me, she loves me in her special way, and she says sweet nothings that make me sway, she does make me grin from ear to ear, with her special loving that no ruler can number, waking up with her is a brand new day

I thank her for saving me from myself, my days of being blue are years away, that waking up alone is not to be, because in my past you walked on in, loving me for me, with all of my quirks, with you in my life, every day on the calendar is a brand new day

My Best Friend

They have always been there for me throughout my life, I've been lucky in that way, at almost every phase of my life, someone who I could count on to have a couch to sleep on, money to borrow, a ride when needed and lots of fun to be had

The first one I've known all my life, a medical man now, a hockey player for life, we were inseparable in our little neck of the woods, come a new season, come a new sport, always a stick or ball in hand, hunting the neighborhood or kicking a can, there were lots of laughs and plenty of sleepless overnights, where plans were made and our dreams were laid out for the rest of our lives

In a new address in a new land, I met him, the kid all the girls loved, oh how the girls swooned all over my friend, at times, I get the girl who would always be at the end, I'll always be forever grateful to my generous friend, not just for the girls but his generosity of his heart and without him I would never have known about my favorite band

Mutt and Jeff, that's what we were called, him seeming seven feet tall and me, we'll just say I'm small, but oh what fun we had traveling this land, going from state to state following our favorite band, the fun that we had cannot be measured, the tales of travels forever written in the sands, tie dye smiles moving with the wind

My last and best of them all, is the women I wake with, yes she is my lover but more important than that, she is my best friend, the best I've ever had, she has seen me at my worst and she has seen me at my best, she knows me inside and out, she loves me for me, warts and all and for that I'm and grateful as my life moves along

My Feelings For You

I'm so happy that you are my wife.
you make me so happy, I don't deserve you,
to have you in my life, you fell in love
with me and I'm grateful for that every day

I couldn't ask for a better friend, lover and wife,
carrying our child, our beautiful family becomes
complete, a son for us, a brother for my son
and another branch of life from your beautiful soul

I thank you for all your support through good times and
bad, I feel your love wherever I go and I always spread
the gospel of you, I brag about you to everyone and every
positive word has been earned by you, I love you, and it
makes me so happy that it is you that I see first everyday

I Love You So

I know you think this is about girl, but you would be wrong, it is a love affair I've had my whole life, it makes me cry and laugh, it makes me happy and sad, it also makes me shake my bones and tap my toes, it has made me cry and it has been there when love was in the air

The first time I heard you I was just a boy, seasons in the sun and I was hooked for life, I would never be the same, a song had affected me, made me think and filled my soul and I knew I wanted more, I was hooked and I would jones until I had more, so much more

Growing up, you've been with me in my heart and soul, you've been with me in good times and bad times, with me at my best and with me at my worst, you've been there my whole life, you were there when I made love for the first time to my wife

The best was when the man with the most beautiful sound, a sound that only a god could help make, came into my life, a sound so beautiful, a smile comes across my face, a sound that has so affected my life, moved me forward and made my life shine so brightly, I share him with my sons and wife

I listen to you wherever I am, when I get up in the morning until I go to sleep, from the first day I heard you and I'm sure to the day I die, you make me feel things that I can never explain, a big pile of feelings that put a smile on my face, I've danced in stores and sung out loud while standing in place

I know this sounds silly but I don't really care, I'm taking you with me when I die, while I lie in my casket, I want headphones in my ears, i-pod on full blast so god can hear me and knows I'm near, uncle Jerry playing and me without a care, here I come lord with a smile on my face

Lying With You

As I watch you undress, a smile beams across my face, seeing the body I want to caress, you walk towards our bed, the place that is only our own, I feel your warm body as I'm lying with you, your flesh touches mine making fireworks go off in my head

As I'm lying with you, I know there is no better place, our toes intermingle, our legs lie at rest, your calming pace calms down my racing heart, everything is how it's supposed to be, you lying next to me, on top of me, me lying there with happiness on my face

When we are in each other in body and soul, I feel your warm love spread all through me from my head to down to my toes, like a new morning, a new day where nothing can go wrong, just you and me, in our own world, even if it's just for a little while

While the world throws distractions trying to take us out of our happy place, I can always go where we know life is at its best, lying with you, while you're lying with me, looking at your green eyes, I'm always at rest, holding you close, holding you so tight you run out of breath, your heart holding mine in our favorite place

Brothers In Life

Throughout my life I've been lucky, to have had all of you there to protect me, help me, grow with me and be there when I was at my best and worst, none of you really knew each other, me meeting you at all different phases of my life, from birth to today

This is not about my blood brothers, I really have nothing nice to say about them, I'm ashamed to say that they are the seedy people of this world, stealing, lying, violence, never helping others, taking money from a sister when she had none to give

My real brothers, people who know me, have been there for me my whole life, knowing my fears, and oh yes, we had lots and lots of fun, touring with our favorite band, playing sports and going to the beach just to watch the girls with a wink in our eye

Some of you I have not seen in years, life has gotten in the way, some of us have moved away, new wives, children have arrived, but in my heart you will always be there with me, as I watch the game and play our favorite music loud with a smile on my face

My Favorite Song

You know it when you hear it, the way it makes you feel, your heart gets warm, your legs move a little, a smile comes across your face, you involve yourself in the words, it sings to you when it's your favorite song

I've had a few over the years, Seasons in the Sun was my first one, then came along The Last Song, I remember lying in bed, feeling good listening to their melody, I remember the summer, listening to my favorite song

As I got older, I was torn between Mandy and Rock Steady, my tastes were changing, feel good melodies to loud obnoxious guitars, my hair was long, the bass was loud, the speakers were shaking from my favorite song

In my freshman year, he was introduced to me and is with me to this day, the sweet sound of his guitar, the story telling voice, Comes A Time until I die, when only love can fill, I miss the man who sang my favorite song

Sowing For Love

Is it me or does love seem to be going extinct? As I'm watching the world, the sadness life brings, here in my homeland and out in the rest of the world too, everyone only seems to care about getting theirs and always being right, no one stops to sow for love

The talk is that we are all created equal, but no one really thinks that, please don't tell me you do, life doesn't lie, I see the results and it's kind of sad that we don't practice what we preach, everyone laughs at everyone's weaknesses instead of offering a helping hand and settling our differences, we all need to stop and think and sow for love

I'm lucky I know, there is love in my home and my love and I try to help others as much as we can, others should follow our lead, not just help the ones they know, but to help all of our fellow man, if we keep going down this path, we will cease to exist, so it won't even matter because there will be no love to sow

Love has to be spread, Love has to be grown, spread around to each other before our world is no more, stop the wars, stop the killing, man can be kind if they stop always wanting more, we must change course and take the road not taken because of the road we have chosen love will refuse to grow

My Favorite Place

The second week in August is one of my favorite times of the year, pack up the family and off we go, going to a place of solitude, a place we call home if only for a little while, with my favorite people in all of this world

When we go to the town next door, it is full of color, food off all kinds, music in the air, everyone a little different, sitting on a bench watching the actors doing their thing while ice cream falls down my little one's face

I love this week visiting with our giant friends under the sea, while the seals pretend to be our friends acting like they want to play until we get too close, so they swim out of sight to where we can't see, laughing at us on their way

The best part is an Irish beach, the beach is so perfect, just like a Monet painting, the sounds of children laughing, a wonderful peace with the sea pounding the sand, sand dunes all around, the breeze in my face, this is my favorite place

You Need
To Help Yourself

I know I could never understand, I've never stood in your shoes, having others judge me by the color of my skin, look down on me because they think they are better because they are white, I know I've never been there and I hope there will be a day when that all ends

I write this for you because I need to make you understand, you need to help yourself, don't take any shit from the south, but you need to vote, make your kind understand, that if you don't vote, you'll never feel like this is your home, your land

When I see and hear about Chicago, I know this isn't you, just bad seeds that others perceive to be you, but you need to change that view, it's not something I can help you with, only your kind can do it and that starts at the voting booth, this is how you become the man

I know your history, horrible doesn't even come close to what happened in the past, there have been many times in history when I have hated my own kind, I hear what red states say about the man in the white house, it makes my blood boil, it makes me hate the white man

In the end though, it is only you who can help yourself, get organized in the south, fight for your rights, show everyone that what is mine is yours and don't take shit from any white man, be civil, be smart, get out and vote, make where we live your land

My Next Door Family

I think of you often, because when I do, I smile, my dirty face at your door on a daily basis, always welcomed with a smile and a cucumber sandwich, a voice that sounded angry but my young ears knew all the words that came out were backed with love

I never told you how I felt but I think you knew because I was at your house every morning, trying to look my best on Sundays because you would fill my belly until the food came out of my toes, a silent deal that was made as we went to church

You knew I was poor and you were not, but you never judged me, hugs were handed out by the mom, while I sat and watched TV with the dad, eating on tray tables, watching the "Thriller in Manila", always feeling that I had a warm home to go to

As the years moved on, I never forgot about you, it made me sad when the dad passed away, I always remember his grumbling with a smile, you meant so much to me, you always gave this little boy a second home and many happy memories when they were often hard to come by, this poem is for you

When Will We Love Again?

When will we love again, when will we stop all the wars, is it too late for our leaders to realize that we are god's chosen ones, or is his love gone, we must love one another or we will cease to exist making our lord start all over again, to fix the errors of his ways where we the people will no longer lead but never to be born

When will we realize that the world is falling apart and it's because the leaders we allow to lead can't even lead themselves, they point their fingers trying to blame one man when it is all of us who are to blame because we put our faith in leaderless beings who only care for themselves and the people who fill their pockets

When will we start loving one another the way god intended, please don't let him take us off like a coat never to keep us warm again, being done with us throwing us to the side, because once again, man has sinned, being the embarrassment we are, he can't take much more, the day of reckoning is coming if we do not change

When will we love again, when will man know that the only true power is love and not the pain that he spreads, killing innocent people because he is so vain, thinking the pain that he spreads makes the people love him, but it is only fear that they feel with their fake smiles they show while he sits on his pedestal not seeing their pain

We need to start loving again or the world we wish we had will be gone forever, maybe it is meant to be, man destroying man, with god letting nature take over, nature being the only true love he has ever had, bursting with color, smells of wonder and songs from all the special species that is not man, just living and going along for the ride loving each other while leaving man far behind

Music Without You

I didn't know what music was until you came into view, what I thought was music was just filler to my ears, then you came along and showed me the way music should be from an imagination deep in your soul turned into words and sang out to me that only love for the song can fill

You started a genre that is so strong today, your vibe intertwined in all of their souls, the music they sing began with you, carrying your songs to the rest of the world, they sing it with pride all because of their love and respect for you

The sound that came from your guitar was all brand new, a sound no one had heard before, but we all knew it was special and would go on for years, the angels in heaven were jealous of your sound because they knew god was listening to your very sweet sound

When I heard you had passed my heart sank like a stone, never to hear you live again and hear your beautiful tone, I would have to move on and accept the truth but deep in my heart you are not really gone, because I have your music and I can always sing along

There Is No Difference

Let me start with this, they are all liars, there is no difference between the parties involved, they only care about themselves, the power they can gain, how can they divide us, lining their pockets with our money

They start every sentence with "I speak for the American voters", no you don't, you speak for a small group of whack jobs who follow every word you say because they can't think for themselves, mindless followers

It's an honor to represent us, not a lifelong job, but they can't help their greed, they promise the goodies but never deliver, their words don't match their deeds, smiling in their suits filled with lobbyist money, ignoring our needs

We are to blame, instead of electing you and me, we hire lawyers and their friends, the worst of our kind, so next time you are at the ballot box, remember their side is the same as your side until we have the courage to change

The Lost Nomad

From Franklin to Uxbridge, from town to town, from here to there, from nowhere to eternity, life is not fair, the sooner learned the better one is, as the suburban deserts fall asleep, souls are just as lost as the coyote's home, which only the Lost Nomad knows as he wanders around

Being alone is not very fair, the feeling of loneliness a man grows tired, is life worth living when only your footsteps are heard, sitting on rocks with no one to share, dreaming a dream when your love is not yet found, these are feelings only Lost Nomad knows

You can't live by hope because hope is not to be found, when you turn and look around and you only feel frowns, but it is not frowns that you see but the unknowing of eyes that don't recognize the Lost Nomad when he is around

My Three Loves

You are the reason I get up everyday
You are the reason I dream at all
Without you I am the poorest of the poor
With you there is no richer in the world

When I see you conquer your obstacles and fears
The pride in me is so wide, the ocean has no space
When I see you cry, I cry with you, your pain
Is my pain, we ache together through the troubled times

Yes we fight, yes we say things that should never be said
We curse, we yell, things that we could never mean
Because love is not perfect, love has its bad days too
We fight the bad days because the good days will be here
soon

There is no love stronger than ours, because it is true
My heart has no room for others, I breathe because of you
I live because of you, you are my blood, friend and my
lover we are family, what I had always heard it should be,
you are what I've been searching for all of my life, my
three loves

The Danger Of Words

Do they know what they are doing, do they know what they are saying, do they understand their words are causing grave danger, and they tell lies based on what side you are on, keep telling them until they are no longer lies

They can't admit they bit off more than they can chew, their dangerous words which they spew cannot be taken back because they are not new, and they have their flock following every word that they say, keep telling those lies until they are true

Their side your side but they don't understand we are living in a time where violence is right around the corner based on what they say, they open their mouths but they don't care that their dangerous words are causing us to live day to day in despair

We live, we breathe and we give a damn that their lies that come so easy will not be tolerated anymore, because words can be dangerous if we let this go on so give them the word that trumps above all, love is the word that we shall all live by because God does not give his blessing to those who cause war

Nobody's Perfect

Life is hard enough without being perfect, always looking good, perfect hair, perfect teeth, perfect clothes, perfect weight, perfect everything from your head to your toes, trying to be perfect every day is a full-time job, just ask yourself, do I shine like a perfect diamond or an ugly looking toad

Your television has you thinking that you're too fat, too short, too tall, too small, too skinny, too bald, your clothes are ugly and so are you, you don't have a gold toilet, what's wrong with you, why can't you be perfect like the beautiful people are, their shit doesn't stink and they only crap gold

Well if you ask me, being perfect is overrated, living up to standards that no one can attain, always looking good, having perfect teeth and having to smell good all the time, I'll take my life, my crooked teeth, my frumpy sweats and my bald head, watching my favorite team and wondering what that smell is

The Magic Box

I'll be honest, I still don't understand it completely, but I love the way it feels, I still remember when I touched it for the first time, I know I wasn't doing it right, I was scared of it, wondering what was I supposed to do with the magic box

As I got older, the girls I was with would teach me how to handle it, what felt right and not so right, I knew as I went along to listen for the sound, I can't really explain it, but if you listen closely, the sound explains itself from the magic box

When I became an adult, I always had a mission, treat it right, there will be rewards for you after, get lazy and I was on my own, it's mystical and delightful and many other feelings that abound, many special woman with their special magic box

I only have one today, no more seeing how many I can pleasure, that one I have now is the best, I know the movements, I know its sound, I know when it's angry and I know when it's wants me around, yes it's that special, my very own magic box

My Boys

I look at my boys and thank the sky above because they are so beautiful, healthy and wise, I'm not my father, I would die for my boys, I will protect them until they become men and ready to go out on their own

Watching them grow has been a godsend, from watching them first walk, to their first words, to my first son picking up a guitar to my little one adding numbers like he's been doing it is whole life, this is all magic to me

Over the years be it summer, spring, winter or fall, I've watched them grow into wonderful human beings, they care about others, always willing to lend a helping hand, with a smile on their face and goodness in their heart

Not every day is the best, we have our lousy days, yelling and saying things we don't mean, those days are few, I love giving a life I never knew, making them happy and them knowing that they are loved through and through

Our Anniversary

I've been trying to figure out
what to say in a poem for
our anniversary, trying not
to repeat myself from past words

Then I thought that the only
words I can think of is you
are my best friend, you make me
so happy and I love you

Four years seems like forever in a good way,
feeling I've known you my whole life, thinking
where would I be without you, sometimes wondering
if you are just a wonderful dream I'm having

No words, no matter how many there are,
can express how I feel about you, how much
my heart is filled with the thought of you, every
hour of every day since you entered my life

Touring With My Friends

Get up, get out of bed, it's time to go see my favorite band, my friends in the driveway beeping the horn, yelling for me not to forget my head, a loud laugh is heard, smiles all around, it's time for touring with my friends

The East coast cities await, from Providence to New York, from Boston to PA our trunks filled with beer, tie dye in the wind, a shit eating grin from ear to ear, I look all around, everyone with smiles, not a frown to be found, it's touring with my friends time again

The music fills my soul as well as my friends, all sharing this special time, our thoughts being controlled by the magic that we've been fed, twenty thousand strong cannot be wrong, this is the place to be when I'm touring with my friends

We pack up our bags, somber moods in our heads, this tour is over, reality setting in, our offices and desk await, so we can make our bread, until we hear the word that the boys are going out on the road again, I sit and smile, knowing that soon I'll be out touring with my friends once again

My Sweetest Jelly

You have the sweetest jelly I have ever tasted, your jelly is so sweet the honey bee is in envy, men do the wildest things to have your jelly near, the way you move, the way you smile, the way you sway when you are on your way

I have your jelly in the morning, your jelly at night, I want to have your jelly all the time it makes me so bright, your jelly in the afternoon is such a delight, I crave it all day, I crave it in my dreams, if I could I would have it all the dates in all the months, with the extra day in May

My sweetest girl with the sweetest jelly, my insides moan when you are around, my engines roar at the mere mention of your name, your scent sending young men to meet their judgment day because they will do anything to have your jelly near

Yes Mr. Judge I did the crime that I have been blamed but I did it for the sweetest jelly, the jelly that no man can turn down, the jelly that all men dream of, the sweetest jelly there is, jelly that sends men to break rocks for the man

The Mother
I Never Knew

I realized after you died that I never knew you, the mother of my birth, but your footsteps I've never known, I wish you could be living in yesterday's tomorrow so I could get to know you more to find out the roads you had taken

I never knew your dreams, your wants, your fears, I always wondered what they were through the years, because of your difference we never drew close, you were better suited for only one side of our clan, they were more like you

Your were the strongest person I've ever known but gaining that strength you had to go through so much sorrow, sorrow I wish I had known, your shell was all that I knew, I wish I had more time with you and I would give anything to have that time to borrow

I know you're looking down at me forgiving me for my sin, my sin of not knowing you better, knowing my own mother, the world you lived in wasn't very fair but when it is my turn to go, you I will follow so we can be mother and son again

Our Day

On this day in history you married me
saved me from going down the road
that led to nowhere, saving me from
loneliness, a feeling that has fallen so many

So when this day comes every year
I know that I'm the luckiest man that
has ever lived, because you saw
something in me that you wanted to call your own

I love you my wife with all my heart,
a love that I could never have for anyone else,
a love so strong that when you are not around
I feel all alone, pining for you presence

To everyone else, today is just another day
but to me, it was a re-birth, a new life
with a woman who loves me for me
the way that I love her

The Meaning Of Love

Love is a word that many people just toss around, losing its meaning, treating it as just another word in the dictionary, not realizing the power this one word carries, the true meaning of love

I know the true meaning of love, because you bring out the love in me that no other woman has, showing me that the world is a happy place when two people like us have become one

Love is me missing you as you walk out my door, love is you calling me at nine at night and we talk to four in the morning, saying things that only matter to us that most people would consider silly, but it is love

Love is meeting each other's friends and family because they are an extension of us, another branch of our existence that make us special, that special someone that made us fall in love with each other in the first place

Love is MAKING LOVE, being inside of each other like no one has ever made us feel, having our hearts actually touch, our souls all tangled up like silly string, interwoven not knowing where one ends or begins

Love is us, you and I, two people who are willing to become one with each other, willing to let hearts go unconditionally knowing that the other will only fill it with happiness and smiles

Love is you and I, already knowing that we are with our soul mate for life, that on a certain date in our future, you and I will make the ultimate decision, walk down the aisle and became partners for life, the definition of love

The Men On Top

The two men who own all the oil look down their noses at all of us, spending their money trying to tell us how to vote while they fill their pockets on all our mite, laughing and insulting all the way to the bank

The man looks down on Wall Street from his big penthouse in the sky sitting there looking with his dishonest grin, not a care in the world his pockets well lined after his deal with the devil thinking of course he's better than us

The leader of the House looks down the Capital steps, laughing and grinning because his life is all set, with backroom deals and all those free meals, making his decisions not based on the votes from all of us, but for his best friends who put him in his cozy big house

They call them leaders but who do they lead, no not us, they don't care if we bleed, adjusting their cummerbunds and happy with themselves, they will enjoy each other's company as they all go straight to hell

Save You From Me

I say run, go, get away, you do not want my past, I'm embarrassed to say, don't love me the way you want to, go hurry up and get away, my past and my present are something to slay, I need you to save yourself from me

Your luck is so strong but not strong enough, my luck is bad and is made of the strongest stuff, go on, get out, before you are made into me, the black side of my father who is inside of me, I plead with you to save yourself from me

I say this again, I say it from my heart, you need to stay away, get away get a new start, I feel if this goes on, my worst fears will come true, my bad seed will melt into you, my bad luck will make you become me so I beg you again in this poem, please leave and save yourself from me

They Are My Team

They don't get the accolades as the other teams in town but I wouldn't want it any other way, my team belongs to us, real fans, not the pink hats and the band wagon fans the other local teams have, we are with them to the end

They are not the Flying Frenchman or the Broad Street Bullies, they are big, they are bad, and as blue collar as it gets, they are the working man's team, and they have to fight for every inch of respect, earning it every game

From Orr and Espo to Bourque and Neely to Z and Bergeron, salt of the earth type of players, players who play with class and bite, I'm proud that they represent me, playing a real team game, where you need all 20 to win

They are not the team with the pretty boy quarterback in Foxboro or the team that is known for their colored socks and definitely not the team with the shamrock on their chest, they are the bear, the greatest team to ever come out of the Bay State

Taken For Granted

When I see the world that you put in front of me, it only makes me smile, the colors of the rainbow abound all around, the perfumed fragrances that float through the air, and I couldn't ask for a better friend to walk through each day, you sing me songs more beautiful than any song that has ever been written, you never have to worry about me taking you for granted

People take you for granted every day, they poison you, they cut you down, they take your friends and hang them upside down, put them on their walls as trophies explaining that they have to thin the herd, but we all know it's for their own greed and good, saying I do love her, but they really do not care claiming that we can't hurt her because god is her maker

We have to protect our future they say, we can't have our kids inheriting our debt, but they will inherit the world that is on fire because they burn whatever they can find, mold it, drill it, bury it they say, no one will know, everyone is too busy to see and the politicians turn a blind eye with their hands in their pockets, taking you for granted is their way of life

You are my friend and I will stand with you until the day I die, cultivating my home to give you a smile, breathing in your air on a cold crisp day, I look around and I see all your miracles, knowing that I would never lay any pipe to make you cry, because you are my secret love affair that I would never take for granted

When I'm Thinking Of You

It's your birthday once again and here I am trying to figure out what you see in this man, I'm a big disappointment, that I do understand, I walk around all day not liking myself, I brood like an old dog, trying to figure how things went wrong, but then I smile when I'm thinking of you

I keep on telling myself that I'm doing the best that I can, but is this the truth, am I being an honest man, I look in the mirror wishing I could give you things that other men can, the things you deserve, loving you like no other man, but I smile once again when I'm thinking of you

When I look in the mirror I'm not the man I hoped to be, a successful someone walking this land, taking care of his family teaching them to love their fellow man, but this is not the life I had planned, this isn't the life I'm living today and I should do better by you, but then as quick as I'm down I smile once again when I'm thinking of you

Why you love me I'll never understand, I'll just have to believe that I'm blessed like no other man, to have a woman like you fall in love with me is like singing that perfect tune that everyone must hear, so I'll end this poem with these last words, I smile every time when I'm thinking of you

The First Sinners

Adam and Eve were long ago, before Jesus Christ which has led to you and me, lovers, more than friends, lovers for life, which all you who judge, our very first sinners, but judged they are not because it was long ago, so called God's children, the first to sow

Who are you to judge with your own house falling down, your nasty misdeeds that are not unknown, judging us, mocking us instead of looking at your own, who are you to point fingers when you're all alone

I've talked to God and he does not judge, peace and happiness is all he wants, love one another no matter your race, love one another, never feel that you are a living disgrace, you love who you love and you live with a smile, while always knowing that you are the definition of grace

Don't judge me on who I love, but judge me for the man I've become, judge me for helping my neighbor, don't point your gun and act as if you are better, spreading your hate and all of your anger trying to start violence hoping we jump at your bait

Life is too short we only go around once, let's live in peace and with a smile on our face, let's dance and sing, working hard in our lives, helping one another, living this life that we lead, loving who we love and being at peace

You Derserved To Die Young

When it was your turn to go at the early age of sixty, I felt no love, my heart left empty, it was about time I said, your life was useless, I sit here thinking about three of your sons, they know only how to lie, all of them useless and without any sense, you would be so proud they turned out just like you

You did society no favors, you are the one we would have left behind, you begged and you stole while hurting your wife, telling everyone lies to the day you died, you were not missed that is no lie because we all knew you were going to hell and not up to heaven in the sky

You added nothing to our lives, the ten you left behind, in your mind we were just your ten little bastards just taking up your time, while you cheated on your wife with whores you found on the street, us ten little bastards would listen to our mom as she broke down and cried throughout the nights

It's been many nights since you have passed, the father who is the worst, your title now stands, your life just a joke except we who were left behind, I know I will be better, I already have, loving my two sons who I'll never leave behind

The Most Boring Man In The World

Here I am again, hiding from the world with a smile on my face, everyone else wanting everyone to notice them, where they are, what they are doing, look everyone, here I am, but no not me, I'm quite happy being the most boring man in the world

Facebook, Twitter, Instagram, Myspace, texting, no they are not for me, I'm quite happy picking up a phone and talking to my love and just being me, a man quite happy walking in his shoes, holding my wife hand's being the most boring man in the world

I go to work each day, nothing flashy just sitting at a desk and doing my part moving the world to another day, living life a minute at a time, I figure I'm living longer because my days go so slow, my minutes doing a slow climb, just being the most boring man in the world

You watch, you judge me, why won't he come along, come with the rest of us you say, your life is so slow, but that's okay with me, I like my life just fine as long as I'm with my wife, I want to be wherever she is being the most boring man in the world

Scott Bourne

Religion

I want to believe, I really do, but when politicians use it as a scare tacit, in the Middle East, heads are cut off in Mohammad's name, Jews kill Muslims for land that should be shared, how can I believe that religion is the voice of God, when evil is winning

Listen to God or you will die, are these really his words or people who relay their meanings as his words, remember the bible was written by man, men with their own bias, their own agendas, what favored them, these are man's words not God's

What I say many times is not what I think, I do believe in something, just not this made up community that was created by man, Mohammad, Jesus and the One whose name can't be mentioned, my belief if they are real, they believe in peace and love

Growing up I always believed that religion was supposed to be about everything that wasn't evil, but the older I get, no matter what religion there is, people have no problem killing in the name of their God, how can these actions make me a believer

No one knows what any of these Gods think, but I do know that they are ashamed of us, man using his name for their misdeeds, they are judging us and we are failing their true beliefs, Jesus, Mohamad, and the One you can't say want us to stop

Stop using their name for all of your sick ways and beliefs, religion is to teach peace and love, not death and destruction, if the religion I see every day is THE religion, I want no part, I'll put my faith in family because that's all that really matters

I'm learning that what happens here while we are alive on earth is all that really matters, not what happens in death, were you good or bad, did you have a positive impact on society, were you good to your fellow man, this is how I want to be judged

I know that you won't believe me, but I know what God wants and it's not that hard to understand, it make so much sense, it really is this easy, "only leave footprints where you go and love your fellow man/woman", you don't need religion for this, it's that simple

My Religion

My religion shakes my bones, warms my heart and brings a smile to my face every time I hear it, my religion doesn't start wars, fill hearts with hate, and contribute to bigotry showing the worst sides of humanity

From the guitar player in San Francisco to the poet in Minnesota, from the Boss in Jersey to the kid in Sacramento, from the singers in Motown to the Canadian in California to the boys in Liverpool, this is my religion

My religion is about togetherness, not division, filling my heart with a smile, teaching me about sorrow and at the same time opening my eyes to the whole world, that love is everywhere if you are strong enough to find it

My religion is the oldest religion, it has been making people dance and spreading happiness since the beginning of time, no other religion can have such a boast, only my religion can shake you from your head to your toes

Why So Much Hate

What happened to we are our brother's keeper, today it's how we can hurt our brothers and sisters, the news pitting us against each other, neighbors don't talk, and distrust is everywhere, criticize until we feel the pain, why is there so much hate in this land

God's gospel is to love and be kind to each other but the parishioners don't practice what they preach, they judge by how you look, what it's in your pocket, what can you do for me, why is there so much hate in this land

Love should be able to conquer all, but god's love is worn like clothing, taken off when they are done, but god's clothes should always be on, because god's work is never done, why is there so much hate in this land

Hate is what we are now, but not what we have to be, hate is the enemy, but love is what we want to be, have to be, need to be, why is there so much hate in this land

I look in my family's eyes to see the love that wakes me every morning, then I look into my mirrors eyes, searching for love in the world that is not there, may the love of our future children conquer the hate of today's leaders, why is there so much hate in this land when only love can conquer what is at hand

Solitude

Solitude has two meanings based on who you ask, solitude can be heaven, never having to share your soul, or solitude can be a prison, looking for love and having no one to share it with, two meanings for a word that is all alone in its being, a word to itself

Solitude to some is a life of happiness, to those who grew up with too many people in their homes where nothing was theirs and everything had to be shared, they see being all alone as heaven, their time is theirs, to be alone and just look at the stars

Solitude to some is hell, always alone, no one to share your life with, no brothers, no sisters, always being your own team, where happiness is in a shopping line where contact with people brings a smile, going to a game so thousands can be their friends

Solitude is a powerful word, a word that can bring a smile to your face or burn in a hole in your soul, a word has different meanings to those who live in the city or live on a farm, sitting on a mountain or sitting on a beach watching the waves go by

Scott Bourne

I'm one who doesn't like solitude, I've been alone at times in my life and solitude wasn't my friend, I like the noise of music, my wife's hand in mine and my kids all around even if they are being too loud, I'll take my life filled with people and sound

I'm Not A Perfect Man

I'll be the first to say, that I'm not a perfect man, trust me, I'm no saint, just ask my former partners, they'll give you all the time in the world to explain why I'm not a perfect man, I do though, try to do the best that I can, day in and day out, as I walk this land

I've never gone out of my way to hurt anyone, my father and brothers I'm not, but mistakes I've made are plenty, ignoring sound advice because I know better than all, my judgment has not always been the best, the pain I've gathered has been earned

There are those I've left behind, women I've hurt and friends' bridges that have been burned, but I cannot go back in time and fix my past, life isn't that kind, I just admit that I'm not a perfect man and move on with my life and be the best that I can

None of us is perfect, not even God, like me, he has made his share of mistakes, but we learn and move on and accept our fate, moving on to the next step in our lives, I have sinned, some of my own design, some from bad luck because perfect I'm not

The anger I carry at times takes over my life, fuels the bad decisions I've made, keeps my mind working overtime, keeping me up at night, has lead me to say things that I could never mean, stupidity winning hand over fist, I'm no perfect man

I'm not a liar, but honest to a fault, when I should be silent, I hurt others with my truth, hurting others the result, never realizing that my own truths could be lies to others, I should stop and listen, an art I forget at times because I'm not a perfect man

I'm a father, a husband and an imperfect man, I have had my share of failures, but my life goes on, learning from the best to listen more and understand, like all of mankind should, love the ones I'm with, smile more, knowing that I'm not a perfect man

We are all born to die, so live life to the fullest.
Wherever you go, only leave footprints and love
your fellow man/woman.